Employee Recruitment

B. Vincent

Published by RWG Publishing, 2021.

EMPLOYEE RECRUITMENT

First edition. June 23, 2021.

Written by B. Vincent.

Also by B. Vincent

Bridge Pages
Business Acquisition
Business Bogging
Marketing Automation
Better Meetings
Conversion Optimization
Creative Solutions
Employee Recruitment

Employee Recruitment

Peter Schutz once said hire character train skill, and Henry David Thoreau tells us, do not hire a man who does your work for money, but him who does it for the love of it. Hiring new employees is arguably one of the most important responsibilities in your business. If you buy a bad fax machine, you can replace it. If you choose a bad office building, you can move. But when you bring another human being onto your team, you're introducing something into your company's DNA that will have direct and long-lasting impacts on your team, your reputation and your entire corporate world. Clearly, there is very little room for bad choices here. So how do we get this right the first time? How do we make sure we're hiring talented people who are not just good at their job, but who have personal attributes that will positively impact our workplace? And this course we're going to show you how to do exactly that.

19 percent of employers claimed that applicants lacked skills and experience needed to excel in a 2016 survey. However, in that same survey, 40 percent said they had been experiencing great difficulty filling job positions. In a more recent survey in 2019, seven in 10 companies reported a talent shortage, this level is said to have more than tripled since a decade ago. In addition, more than 50 percent of all existing organizations around the globe have difficulty retaining their employees. These statistics

show that employee recruitment is an increasingly important area that businesses should focus on. Our course is going to consist of a series of critical discussion points, these are designed to cover this broad topic as thoroughly as possible to encourage growth in these vital areas and to facilitate a real and fruitful discussion within your organization about how you can each improve on this essential characteristic, both at work and in your personal lives in general. Some of these will be pretty lengthy and some will be relatively straightforward and brief. At the very end of this roadmap comes the most important final step.

Discussion time, do not skip this, this is the most important part of this training, when you finish this course, you need to spend at least an hour or so going over the questions we supply at the end of the group. Whoever's the head honcho in the group should designate a facilitator whose responsibility it is that each question is covered and that everyone, time permitting, is able to have their say, make sure all contributions are valued, all suggestions considered, and all opinions respected. So let's move into the first discussion point. Take advantage of referrals, referrals are a way to cut out the middleman, in this case, recruiters, when it comes to hiring, who better to talk about the ins and outs of your company than the people who actually work there? Not only do referrals guarantee the employee is sending someone they know fits the bill of what your company's looking for, but it guarantees that they're sending someone trustworthy. With this kind of system in place, there's not much need to pay a recruiter for their services. But don't just let your employees off with a tell your friends award. A certain incentive for every person they refer to that actually gets accepted. It would be best to use a survey about rewards they most desire. But here are a couple of rewards. Ideas for successful referrals. A couple of days paid vacation, a trip out of town to a particular resort, a gift card for a partner and spa recognition during a monthly meeting or in the company newsletter, etc.. A set monetary incentive. Short and sweet job descriptions, job descriptions are vital in the hiring process, they're meant to real potential applicants in. So you have to be impactful, distinct and allude to your company's personality. But you also don't want to risk boring or even confusing a potential employee. You have to hold their attention until they reach the end of your job description, at which point they've already decided that they would love to be the one to fill the position. It's recommended to use 700 to 2000 characters. This forces you to lay out what your company needs, plain and simple. Give the candidate a great application experience, the applicant's experience is crucial, you're basically giving them a taste of what's to come once they pass the application process, treat them with courtesy. In fact, treat them the same way you treat a customer or client. The applicant should get the impression that you care deeply about your people, regardless of whether they're an aspiring employee or a longstanding one. Your first impression with them should stick in such a way that because of their superb experience with you, they'll still maintain that sterling opinion. Even when they get rejected. The candidate or candidate will be so wowed by your professional yet pleasant handling of your experience that they may even spread the word to some friends, friends who might actually fit your requirements better. Here's a couple of ways to help you build rapport with your job seeker. Respect their time, be on time for meetings, be they in person or otherwise, if certain factors are going to keep you from doing so, inform them as soon as possible of the delay. Be a great host, ensure the applicant's comfort, especially if it is a face to face interview. Be as transparent as you can with them. Make them feel that there are questions and concerns matter and when possible, provide feedback to the applicant.

Keep previous candidates in mind, if a candidate doesn't make the cut. You don't have to shred or delete their resumes, keep them around, instead revisit them after a couple of months have passed. More likely than not, the applicant has gained skills that they didn't have the first time around, skills that could be very useful to the company. Moreover, a previous amiable rejection would help the second interview along more smoothly. Make use of social media, job boards are incredibly helpful in generating interest and an ample pool of candidates, though, you don't necessarily have to go to online job boards or Web sites to post your advertisements. You can post them on a social media platform and still get a lot of attention. Here are a couple of suggestions to make your company brand more visible. Check out your audience. Demographic as well as trends. Encourage your employees to promote activities or events on social media. They may also share posts calling for applications. Post a short attention grabbing video about the company posted eye catching job advertisements on social media, you'll needit to go along with the written details. Get your staff involved in drumming up interest, you can ask your employees to help out when drumming up interest, especially on social media. They're able to share things related to the company, such as its activities. This gives potential applicants a glimpse into what their life at the company might be like. You can also get your interns in on this to the main difference between them and your preexisting employees is that they aren't usually paid to make it worth their time. Give them a token of appreciation when a referral turns out successful. Get incentive with your call for applications, not everything about business has to be just business. Get creative, do something such as an Easter egg hunt or a lottery draw.

Prizes can include company merchandise or items with the company logo on them. Feel free to do anything you can think of, provided that it isn't too off brand for your company and isn't too much of a burden on finances. However, be warned, some companies don't always gain a great deal of applicants through this method.

Still, if done right, it can generate a fair amount of attention in the world we live in today that can give you a leg up in the race to hire the best of the best. Here are some out of the box strategies to let people know you're hiring. Post a puzzle, a riddle or a treasure hunt of some sort. Have contests or tests of skill related to the position you're hiring for. Plaster your ads on the sides of vehicles, put up a billboard.

Get yourself on a podcast detailing your company, its work culture, branding and of course, benefits. Grab attention with quirky Wi-Fi names that subtly detail what you're looking for and who to go to. Employer branding, having a reputation for being an excellent employer will give you an edge, you don't need to expend too much effort searching for applicants because they're the ones flocking to you.

[00:11:22] You'll notice that they will be quite engaged, as you have already made a case for being a company that will take good care of them. There are many ways to get your brand across. You just need your phone camera and a message about your branding. Also, employees can write up articles for certain sites detailing why your company is such a great place to work. And there are many ways you can get your brand out there. So make sure to use them to the fullest and control the narrative regarding why your company is indisputably the best. Company culture. You have to show what your company's all about and not just the business related matters, either, you've got to make your company palatable and attractive, not only to potential applicants, but also the employees that are already working for you. Your employees are an important part of the company. And what's more is they can give back by sharing to job seeking hopefuls what it's like to be a part of a company with a culture like yours. So as for finding your company culture, you must evaluate your goals, your vision and mission and work from there. Your benefits will reflect your company culture. But here are a couple of examples. An ergonomic workspace, up to date strategies and office equipment. Ample paid vacation time, regular events that show appreciation for the employees having clubs or groups for employees to socialize with each other.

Bring your non hr staff into the hiring process, human resources doesn't have to handle every little thing about the hiring process. Employees outside the department are also capable of providing help. This doesn't mean that every single person in the company should weigh in on every single applicant. But Nanahara employees are very much capable of providing insights as to what skills are needed around the office. Here are some other ways Nonaka personnel can be of use. They can recommend certain people to the company similar to referrals, they can volunteer to review candidates and their details, which will lighten the load of the staff, they can conduct interviews as well. The applicants shouldn't have to toil through your process if your application process has way too many components or needs far too much information. There's a chance that your applicants might just give up halfway through, filling out applications and go somewhere else, somewhere that isn't a complete slog to apply for. You can't readily expect someone who isn't even part of your company to put in the work after all. Cultivate a candidate pool of less than common personnel as of late, more unconventional work arrangements have arisen and oftentimes they work in favor of both the employer and employee.

Such arrangements allow for greater flexibility, not to mention it allows some leeway for people who may not necessarily have the time to work. The usual nine to five consider hiring remote employees. These employees do require a bit more in the way of organization, so there must be a system in place in order to handle them efficiently. Part timers, because sometimes full employees are costly, costly to search for and hire and also train. Freelancers, these people usually have quite a bit of work experience under their belt and will be a wonderful addition to the team. Consider diversity, consider diversity in terms of who you're considering for your company. Sure, you need a team of people who can fulfill roles that you've laid out on your advertisements, but you should still maintain an open mind and extend the opportunity for a wide range of people to apply for your company. Just because someone hails from a vaulted university doesn't always mean they're the perfect hire for a position. Grit, wit and determination can win out over what's written on the resume. Having an employee who can do what needs to be done is just as important as having someone who knows the industry like the back of their hand. Check out parts of candidates.

Passive candidates are people who aren't actively searching for a job, usually due to the fact that they already have one, maybe they aren't looking in your general direction. A great way to get yourself on their radar is to use social media. You may have to do a bit of waiting, but for the right applicant, it'll be worth it. Invest time getting to know universities around you or their universities in your area, then you need to start rubbing elbows with them as soon as possible. If you create partnerships with colleges or universities, then you can get access to the freshest grads on the market. In some cases, there have been some institutions that made arrangements with colleges or universities in exchange for shouldering course costs. They're given first pick of the letters graduates. Network at various kinds of events, hold or visit events to network prospects, will be able to see you out of the office and you can interact with them in a more casual setting. You can see for yourself if the person you were conversing with is a good fit for your company, whether it be in terms of skills or personality or even both. And as for the applicant, they will be compelled to put a face to your company, therefore giving it a more human element.

You'll remember that particular person when they inevitably come to your company for an interview, especially if you got along like a house on fire and on the applicants end, they'll relish the chance to work with you. Even if certain people don't end up applying for your company during or after the event, they may remember you at another time in the near future. Here are some ways to get your foot in the door. Visit job fairs at colleges or other institutions, show up to business meeting events, especially those which are relevant to your industry, have an open house day or days for people to come and see what the company has to offer. Have a couple of employees serve as volunteers for a good cause. Frequent other professional events or activities. Make use of the mobile in this day and age, people tend to use their mobile phones more than their laptops or tablets or PCs capitalize on mobile, and you might just be able to snag some real talent provided they can connect to the Internet. A person can find out a lot about your company on their mobile phones. An applicant may not directly apply for a position at your company via mobile, but they can save the company website for later and follow through with the application process on another device. So don't slack on your mobile web pages. Hire internally. Before you consider hiring someone from outside your company, someone you don't entirely know, except for a couple of forms, emails and some video or audio calls, consider hiring from within the company. The perfect candidate for the position you are thinking of could be right under your nose, hiding in plain sight. All it takes is just one internal advertisement. Besides, your employees are sure to be grateful for your kind consideration in hearing what they have to offer. Or. Make use of digital recruiting tools. There are dozens of tools you can use at any stage of the recruitment process. So whether it's considering who you want to have for a phone interview, figuring out who's got the most pertinent skills for the position, checking the results of a pretest or checking out someone's references, there's a tool for everything and we mean everything.

Just check out some of the myriad functions for the tools in use today, hosting live meet ups or Q&A sessions to drum up interest, especially in passive candidates keeping your Web sites and or Web pages up to date, checking a job seekers background and references, having video interviews, tallying who the best applicants are with rubrics and scorecards, establishing your online presence via social media and some online groups examining the skills of applicants such as programing challenges or tests during the application process. Testing an applicant psychometrics to evaluate their personality traits, collaborating on the hiring process. Checking via survey. If a candidate was satisfied by their interviewing experience, sharing employee experiences on review sites to provide insight into the company, sourcing the applicants, keeping track of the applicants, contacting prospective candidates, looking into applying predictive analytics during the hiring process, using learning tools to help impart skills or knowledge that will help your newly minted employees get used to the job. Having social recruiting software that'll take care of some, if not all, of the tasks for you. Offer equal, if not better, pay and benefits. Imagine that you have an applicant on your hands, someone who really gets the company and what its goals are, has the right skill set, has ample years experience, is willing to start immediately and is otherwise the absolute perfect fit for the job.

But then one day they call you saying they found a position at Company X Y, you ask them and they respond because they simply just pay better. Obviously, it's a situation you want to avoid a solution to this dilemma is to offer the same pay is Company X. Or you can one up your competitors and offer a little extra extra perks. For instance, to get a more accurate picture of the perks you need, you may take a look at the employee value proposition. Basically, it's what your company offers as an equivalent for your employee skills and hard work.

Evaluate current conditions at the company by asking questions such as how do the staff feel about their salaries? What about their benefits, or are they satisfactory? How do they feel about the company? Do they enjoy working there? How's the work environment? Does the staff have enough freedom and work? Does the staff get rewarded fairly and often? Once you have your parks ready to go, make sure to have them all spelled out in your advertisement. Clearly, yet subtlely. Ensure you have the best pick of applicants in the pool, it goes without saying that it's best to have the best applicants. These, of course, are the ones with years of experience under their belts, the ones with the qualifications, the ones with the top notch achievements. With this, there won't be any doubt about the person you've gotten on board with the company. You'll definitely have an easier go integrating them into the workflow. Or go for the unorthodox picks, alternatively, you could also not look too closely at achievements on paper and instead hone in on qualities that your company needs. Personality traits that fit the company culture may turn out to be a major find. If the potential of a candidate speaks to you.

Don't give anyone else the chance to unlock it. Check references. It is easy for people to cover up past misdemeanors or perhaps falsify records these days regardless. Business is business and you have a company's reputation to uphold check references, check backgrounds, review everything with a fine toothed comb. What you see is what you get. So make sure you're getting exactly what you see on that resume. Don't skimp on off boarding, sometimes we just can't keep our finest or brightest or smartest employees with us, sometimes they just have to leave the proverbial nest for one reason or another. But one thing you can do is ensure that the onboarding process is nice and smooth. You've got to make the employee truly feel that what they've done for the company will always be remembered and appreciated. In the event the resigned employees new job doesn't work out, it could result in said employee returning to the company later on. However, if the off boarding was awkward and difficult for everyone involved, don't expect them to come back.

If they do,then don't expect an easy smile on the returners face, though. If the employee doesn't return to the company, they still might be able to refer new talent because of the sterling off boarding experience. And now it's discussion time, the most important part of this training, whoever's the head honcho in the group should designate a facilitator whose responsibility it is that each of the questions you see on your screen is covered and that everyone, time permitting, is able to have their say. Make sure all contributions are valued, all suggestions considered and all opinions respected.

Don't miss out!

Visit the website below and you can sign up to receive emails whenever B. Vincent publishes a new book. There's no charge and no obligation.

https://books2read.com/r/B-A-QWUO-XZTPB

BOOKS 2 READ

Connecting independent readers to independent writers.

Also by B. Vincent

Bridge Pages
Business Acquisition
Business Bogging
Marketing Automation
Better Meetings
Conversion Optimization
Creative Solutions
Employee Recruitment

About the Publisher

Accepting manuscripts in the most categories. We love to help people get their words available to the world.

Revival Waves of Glory focus is to provide more options to be published. We do traditional paperbacks, hardcovers, audio books and ebooks all over the world. A traditional royalty-based publisher that offers self-publishing options, Revival Waves provides a very author friendly and transparent publishing process, with President Bill Vincent involved in the full process of your book. Send us your manuscript and we will contact you as soon as possible.

Contact: Bill Vincent at rwgpublishing@yahoo.com www.rwgpublishing.com